OPEN

David & Honor
With Best Wishes
Paul Blount, Sept. 2022

BY THE SAME AUTHOR

POETRY

Wao

Fab

Boo!

tink

Think?

Bugalugs

tree

until

HOODOO

OPEN

by

PAUL BLOUNT

THE CLUNY PRESS
ST. ASAPH
2022

First published in 2022 by

The Cluny Press
Eirianfa
The Roe
St. Asaph
Denbighshire LL17 0LU
Wales

All rights reserved

Copyright © Paul Blount 2022

The right of Paul Blount to be identified as author
of this work has been asserted in accordance with Section 77
of the Copyright, Designs and Patents Act 1988

*This book is sold subject to the condition that no part
shall be reproduced, stored in a retrieval system,
or transmitted in any form or by any means, electronic, mechanical,
photocopying, recording, or otherwise, without the prior permission
of The Cluny Press*

A CIP catalogue record for this book is available from the British Library

ISBN 978-0-9547610-9-7

Designed and typeset by Discript Limited, Chichester
Printed in England by TJ Books, Padstow

DEDICATION

For

Jane

in memory of 36 years

I think I could turn and live with animals,
they are so placid and self-contained,
I stand and look at them long and long.
They do not sweat and whine about their condition,
They do not lie awake in the dark and weep
for their sins,
They do not make me sick discussing their duty
to God,
Not one is dissatisfied, not one is demented
with the mania of owning things . . .

Walt Whitman, 'Song of Myself' (written 1855) pt. 32

Contents

I

Breathe In, In Tens	3
Freud Changed His Brush	4
As A Mucky Pup	5
The Old Men Of Moccas	6
We Sit And Watch Among The Snowdrops	8
Snowdrops, February	9
Fifty Years Ago	10
Jane	11
Girlie Thoughts	12
It Was On An Old Path	14
From The Grey Mare's Tail	15
Lost A Year Of Life	16
March Was A Sad Spring	17
Norman	18
Your Wish	19
Catching The Last Warmth Of The Autumn Sun	20

II

New Birth	23
You Gave Me Blood Money	24
Open The Wheat Chaff	25
Storm Breaking, Daintree Rain Forest	26
In The Iron Age Fort	27
Cry Of The Red-Tailed Black-Cockatoo	28
Wicken Fen	29
Queensland Rainforest	30
The Birdsong Of The Day Birds	31
At The Tableland	32
Salisbury Plain	33
The Gauchos	34
I Have Been To A Place	35
San Francisco	36
It Is Mid March	38
Wormwood	39
Fingerpost Sign	40

III

They Waved White Handkerchiefs	43
The Great US of A	44
I Was Once Asked	45
On The Eve Of A December Divorce	47
In The Leningrad Ice	49
In Vogue	50
All Lives Matter In A Fancy Dress	51
From The Muddy Pond	52
From Leicester To Aberdeen	53
Robben Island, South Africa	54
Fit For Whistler's Brush	56
The Poor Little Things	57
Some Time Ago	60
The Travelling Van	61
Swampy	62
Last Minute Kabuki	63
Her Chemistry	64
Masai	65
She Took A Mazy Run	66
Grenfell Tower	67

IV

Good Friday	71
Anton Webern	72
Returning To Leicester	73
Silks From The Fallen Ship	74
Francis Bacon	75
So She Went To Her Cave	76
We Live On A Land Between The Seas	77
After Schubert	79
Open	80
I Always Liked Georgian Architecture	81
Leicester	82
With Tallis Counting His Latin Notes	83

I

Breathe In, In Tens

'Breathe in, in tens, and breathe out in tens,
and let us sing a lullaby,'
I said to my mother on her death bed.
Remember what the doctor said,
'Breathe in deeply, hold, breathe out deeply.'
She did, and died to the song of a lullaby.

So when my father's time came,
I sang no lullaby, but when he asked
'Do you have a gun?' I talked of Wagner
and the setting sun, and said 'I have no gun'
and he died, also to the song of a lullaby.
Of course, I had lied.

Freud Changed His Brush

Freud changed his brush,
a hog hair as opposed to a sable hair
to enhance your blush
as you recounted a misdemeanour at the country fair.

Bacon could paint eating fish and chips
in a Soho brothel for boys with lots of noise,
discarding soiled canvases in pavement skips.
He studied you wearing a loose scarf;
he liked your poise
but not your fear of losing your mind,
in that parochial slum, sleeping with Eardley
and her squint-eyed boys, starved of scraps,
selling snake juice to dodgy cops
writing their pocket notes checked with rigmarole.

In Glesga speech, what is a book of false knowledge
against our security in a whale of a dream?
Dreams are not straight lines,
but my lines marked your mind to my disgrace
and your face changed in a painted way.

At interview I was asked a question
'Where do you see yourself in five years' time?'
The question placed accents on the weak beat in the bar,
to leave the door ajar.
The Freud in me left me to say,
'I hope in five years' time to be stinking rich,
and probably shacked up to a gold-digging bitch.'
Right answer?

As A Mucky Pup

As a mucky pup she was a girl,
and she a child, and when I held the child
and smelt her kind I knew the pup
would not be blind to reject a pearl,
or say 'No,' to an orderly mind.

Although the smelt kind looked a mess,
dressed as she was in a glamourous dress
of sycamore leaves and muddy streams
which made my dreams come true of you;
she grew into the yew heartwood
and left her childhood cold as frozen snow.

The Old Men Of Moccas

Can I run my hands through your hair
drenched in my love?
Although I am not of your blood,
artistic thought combines between our stream.
You are a slice of time, a present theme
melodious in your wildwood stare,
delicious in what forgot or forgive me not
will be said when read again against a hymn of shame.

History shows we all have shame,
even girls in their giggling swirls
before splashing in the stream
and me drenching my hand in your hair,
drowning me in my dream.

She gambolled into the stream
as I bet on a Prix de l'Arc dream at 8–1
what could go wrong?
A filly with a wonky stead but a beautiful head,
feet all wrong, like a newborn foal,
soaped in coal, tottering on unsprung legs,
alone
it went wet in the head, spunk in the mind
overtrying to be kind.

I, growing back down like the old men of Moccas
languorous, bulbous like the buboes in me,
or you like a hare, scare scented,
lean and jittery, a Buddhist like *satori*.

You could have gone closer to the wind
but not too close to ask that I be like the bourgeoisie
and go down on one knee
to catch the wind from the west,
the south-west, fresh from the sea.
You stank like a skunk when you asked me.

We Sit And Watch Among The Snowdrops

It is snowing in sheets half laundered
by a grey, glaring, gashing sky, grey road dirt muck snow.
Drawn by a Turner line, a fine maunder.

This is first light, so late this perpetual gloom.
Oh, for the boom-bust days of yesteryear,
George W. Bush and Tony Blair,
macho men abloom with votes for dopes
like you and me. The Middle East peace,
a word caught in the snow off-piste.

We sit and watch among the snowdrops
and wait for the quiet of snow stop.

Snowdrops, February

Leave me one snowdrop before you stop time,
so it may go underground in snow time and grow,
and I will sound the cello string, slow
and paint your face in charcoal against the snow.
Play your song for so long as I can hope
to catch your soul and your love of desert sand,
and take your hand
through white marble pillars with red sand veins
and give a subtle squeeze to my last words.

When I looked into your eyes I could not find yourself;
I saw your mother's eyes and the snowdrop,
stoneware pots in a cold white clay glaze.
Stone has a memory left in the vein
and baa baa young, whether bird or bairn,
call for the parent yet again.

Michelangelo worked quarried stone
that night when the moon broke in two.
In a shiver our love broke too.
With fire and a stone axe cut veined gold
toward the moon's ever glow over a snowdrop
never to grow old.

Fifty Years Ago

Walking the water meadow road
I marvelled at the energy of Bach's mighty chords,
played and sealed by midnight frost.
At dawn, I crossed the ford and recalled the loss
new born to me fifty years ago.

Growing through the Finnish spruce,
growing through the heartwood juice,
growing through new growth, my love for you.
You could be so like snow in December
on a cold sea, so self-evident, white.
I always thought you so mercurial,
soft as Janáček in mist moonlight.
The paper on which you wrote became alive,
your porous efficacy soft as Janáček in gloom,
come too soon, too parochial.
I remembered the faces of the saints
held no compassion.

The knot was not kept close and tight,
as in the apple orchard I scarred the apple tree
and creamed the juice freely running down
into Bach's pool of light.
As if in the Amazon, at Manaus,
I had tapped a rubber tree for liquid gold,
when it seemed that nothing moved
and my love was plunged in snow.
I will not let you be that tree that time forgot,
fifty years ago.

Walking the water meadow road,
it seemed everything came from the stars
except love, which was not to be ours.

Jane

I had a friend and she was good and true
and we loved for a moment or two,
and thrilled to young gains, until I found a stray
and we were never joined again
in that grove of olives and dark
scorched singing to the sun.

I took her through a mass of corn
to watch the wolves run across the Siberian plain,
run scared of shadows dismembered from memories gone
quite wild,
and hear Hildegard of Bingen plain song
end the struggle drawn too long.

Girlie Thoughts

First, there was the burning of the old ideas;
then the bees hummed, one bee beside your ear.
I foraged the corn heads from your hair
to separate the palm pulse seed
and make new ideas clear.

There are to be no more girlie thoughts
expressed in pink words about memories.
There will be a fatwa on girlie days out
to shops marked 'Sale', discounted notions
about lost dead words, fluff dressed in mufti.

No more high pitched squeals or bed grunts faked
to appear as IKEA real.
For goodness sake, say something beautiful for once,
leave out the aniline pink dye.
So evermore in the evening sky
gardens will give dreams in delight,
planted with scents perfumed, gloss ridden
with spores strong as morning fresh first light.

When I, a little keen, first overheard
in Drumchapel's shagging field:
'It was nae me that did it,
it waz the big boy who ran away'.

I first watched the Red kite soar into the evening
night air scent. The big boy in his gold and tattoos
high in flight.
If you want pagan talk enter a Drumchapel pub,
engage a big boy and see all sentient go up in smoke,
no girlie talk allowed in here,
we *Rangers* boys rule by fear,

it's in the blood, like puddling the iron,
or when I hold to your face a dandelion
and ask 'No more girlie thoughts
of flight with the Red kite'.

It Was On An Old Path

It was on an old path that I trod
thinking honey words that did not mean a thing;
words with that touch of chic
and firm as pears in a vanilla pod,
a zest of lemon served in Limón,
where the last scar ran against the running stone
as the pigs were slit on December snow,
by the healing well in the Scots machair.

In the land of this nature
Isserlis played his cello
with such elegance as I brushed your hair.
He played a prelude by Bach,
'Because Bach says it all.'
In the mid-January half-light at five p.m.
a blackbird gave its last call,
a cackle like a witches braw.

As a child I had never known touch or kiss,
but with grandma I did bake bread
and could sleep in comfort and love in her bed,
and beside the wet, dark bole in the oak tree.
Forget the conflict of the bad patina of truth,
wishing to be eloquent with legs akimbo.
Leaving her a Gaelic script. A panjandrum in limbo.

From The Grey Mare's Tail

From the Grey Mare's Tail
to the Garden of Cosmic Speculation,
we follow the trail from Loch Skeen
into another timed dream,
where montane willows grow to a pretty show
and provide insulation
to the Iron age Tail Burn fort
with its lost latch an afterthought.

Once you had raided the sweetie shop
it was hard to let go when the jackal
gripped its lips and both went over the waterfall
into that trouble of silence.

To be blunt, from *lunt* to *lunt*
to hunt the sick deer at night
with sloppy language and a rancid flight.
Really, your speculation was not so much cosmic
as comic in the morning new light.
Maybe, you did not catch the latch
to close the door.

Lost A Year Of Life

Lost a year of life,
. . . still alive,
Grandad dead, found cold in bed.
I said to my mammy,
'We are not in a good state. Can I open the door?'
I felt clammy with her mixed messages
lost in the shrubbery,
with nicknames hanging on leaves
as a backdrop to a pretence to grieve,
based on a slogan
written on a blue ribbon that hung from her hair.

Grandma, I was really proud of the way
you carried yourself.
It was me who stole the jam from the pantry shelf.
But confession does not resolve the rhythmic pattern
of deceit, or conceit.

Grandma, can I hold you once more
before I go? No more dialogue, just hold.

March Was A Sad Spring

March was a sad spring, begin in dark
in a noggin of liquor and a carrot egg,
oil drained by midnight.
Stiff in frost and I in lost,
lost for harmony.

When the rodding be done in the high ground
behind the birds' clatter, of this much could I say
in this menagerie of white sound
in the honey bee hive, to overreach an idea
of balancing stones to fit in a Machu Picchu mind
constructed from a doctrine found in Sharia.
The stone to fit razor sharp,
clinked to slit between you and me
as we sailed in the clinker built boat
and sailed too close to the still wind.

Sally ho, no matter what and sealed with what love?
You lost the context, the texture,
I the poster boy cadenza.
My mother's hair woven into the black
goes back a long way, but I cannot see her still
in her root and stem, open to me.
Mother, I do not need words now
as you gave me none.

Norman

Disaffected grew the tumour strong.
'What is right, and what is wrong, after all?'
the snake-oil salesman asked with malignity,
leaving you with no dignity as you bled through every pore.
Grandma held your hand. 'He can still hear,' the nurse said
as Dad called your wife a whore.

I read the scrawlings on the toilet wall,
written in green ink to expose the obscenity of it all.
In the shining light bouncing off the toilet seat
in a hospital ward, with your secrets locked
in a salesman's briefcase, I looked at your face
as you let out that scream and I shut out,
thinking only as a child
of that knickerbocker-glory ice cream,
and the green ink scrawled by Billy the Kid
in a wild west bar.

From Norman stock, what norms held him together now
as he haemorrhaged his secrets and his eternal vow?
as Grandma held her second son's hand.

Your Wish

Your wish was to spread your ashes
as wide as a Smooth-leaved Elm
and as tall as a Snowdrop Tree, a thought
as absurd as rowing reindeer in a sleigh boat.
But you could sketch like a miner underground,
dark and profound.
Your eyeless pain dripping a mile into the earth,
into the still-birth.

So this is what I did.
I went into Rainbow Wood after rain,
in a glade where once fancy fled
and gave a merry chase of the girl
who would become my gyne,
and after the rain as each leaf cooled
by autumn mellowness of our late age,
I laid the ash of you.
One ash on each leaf, and sat on an elm seat
with a hammer shaft and thought the absurd,
that loss could preserve it in a single word.
Love.

Catching The Last Warmth Of The Autumn Sun

Catching the last warmth of the Autumn sun,
a tangy mesh that was tangible at rest;
the airtight intellectual system explained undone.
Your hair tangy in the ploughed sky.
When I saw your ware gleam in the sun
ploughed sky.

Okay name me a love that isn't mistimed,
splashed over crockery like Royal Worcester
or Sèvres gone awry, thrown wrong on the wheel.
Okay what I said was misspelt,
an intellectual system in sun melt.

I questioned if the body can self heal.
Cancer has an odour. Oh dear,
can you smell it in me?
Or can you smell the rumbling horses' breath
against the skaters skrate on the curling pond.
The Tummel tumbling to a final coda,
the sunlight passing over.

II

New Birth

New birth, late March,
the sound of shotgun and rifle fire in the air,
the need to unleash the hounds to course the hare.
What gets into a crazed mind? The killing gene?

In the narrow dene by the larch
no mythological scene or classical frame,
cropped thought like a Mondrian
but nature has no straight lines
just the foeman loading his gun to take aim
with a straight mind,
to make the new still-birth.

You Gave Me Blood Money

You gave me blood money, which I took
to the land of the red kangaroo,
left you a single white pearl covered in dew
and watched butterflies fly over a Queensland brook.

Before birth songlines and ceremonies,
covered in red ochre poured on the red kangaroo
you told me stories in the sand,
in my dreamland at night in Tableland
where it all began one hundred million years ago.

When each cell suggested a sound
universal in its knowledge of itself,
but not to us;
whether bird, leaf, platypus, fig tree,
or your beauty when the raindrop
from the shaped green leaf
dropped on your face to speak to me.

Mr Darwin believed in chance
but man cut his sound in the first rainforest
where Jesus was born to dance
in the land of the Black-Cockatoo.

Open The Wheat Chaff

Open the wheat chaff and drill into the grain,
to release the sentiment febrile
without your own axe to grind.
It is a late November morn with cuckoo spit
still hanging down from the floor,
for you to find all the many acorns
still to fall for god's recall
of his promise tall in years gone by.

But to now, let us decide this Autumn tide
whether he be pride or lost in Milton's book.

Storm Breaking, Daintree Rain Forest

In mumbo-jumbo time, yes Messiaen again,
the frogs will be out hanging on a line,
taut like the Chinaman stretched by his pigtail
at the goldrush time.

Pelts of raindrops dot the Chinaman's eye,
a kangaroo lies speared by an aboriginal arm.
Greedy drops in mumbo-jumbo time,
this time the rain they call the Wet
explodes the sky to forget the black fella
cutting out a note through the throat,
ending the Chinaman's goldrush time
and whoops with the Black-Cockatoo
Messiaen's end time line.

In The Iron Age Fort

In the iron age fort above my home
it is evident that ancient man
had no love of angles or red-tape in mind;
seeing ruins in squares or rectangles, or in an angel
holding a hazel wand with dead men's bells.

The sequestered oak wood of the twisted dwarf oaks
forming a canopy over rock,
moss covered, join this rain-whipped spot
to the yellow-eyed osprey and the whirling
of a maverick Red kite on the westerly wind.

Did ancient man give back his swag?
With the kernel of an idea
that transformed him from the hillfort to my home,
or was the idea put back into his bag
when corrective vision gave him a greater insight,
to flatten the curve drawn by the Red kite?

Cry Of The Red-Tailed Black-Cockatoo

Wake-up call.
He thinks about his pot, today.
A potter with water and red clay,
the Red-tailed Black-Cockatoo;
a potter with prohibitive thoughts,
red water and red berries in his hands.

Under a brise-soleil to protect from the sun
he flew, the queen bee of the tribe,
a striped bee with aboriginal clay marks
rain dropped spotted colours forming blue sky,
drip dropping on to the pot.
Patterned drops off your tongue,
cut in two by the spirit man.

We two, blood brothers now,
can share those prohibitive thoughts
and wash our hands in the wet berries
contained in the clay pot, to the cry
of the Red-tailed Black-Cockatoo.

Wicken Fen

The marshy fenland had all but gone
when we walked alone and met to atone,
toward a oneness and saw the wild swan
isolate, alone in quick flight,
a catch of undertone in harmony.
The fen wind forming our company with the swan.

Because we hid under different names,
names we changed with things unseen
in the wide fen unknown, known and seen
as in a damaged gene.

As in the greed isotope in Homo sapiens,
I, as an atheist want to read the Parish Magazine
and play moves on the chess board
in a secret dene far from the marshy fen,
all but gone with the last Swallow-tail we saw
in a malachite green and lapis lazuli
from Afghanistan which flew with the swan
to search the four treasures we sought,
pellucid and oiled by the swan,
open fully to our view.

Queensland Rainforest

I am hearing owls call above
the Saragossa Sea, rainforest awash with sea.
I am feeling you within me,
making sense of unreality.

I am hearing owls explode their call
and demand, and expect.
I am swimming in the Saragossa Sea,
without feeling you within me.

A torpedo has just struck the ship,
the last merchant in the convoy.

The inner reef and outer reef
washing the Saragossa Sea over me.
The inner grief and outer grief
of never having said, 'I love you,'
of sharing the owls' call.

Messiaen's birds did not sing in chords,
scored in the sandstone strata.
In a cave they hid from the hard rain's pitted spots,
feathers a soft and wet toccata,
like the calling of a strong, strange saxophone note,
hoping.

The Birdsong Of The Day Birds

The birdsong of the day birds was entirely gone
in the wood after dark had stripped their song.
She had a little touch of liquid white
on that night, a voluptuous fair-headed ingénue,
but who could have told you that you were as cruel as Yeats
when he told Maud Gonne,
'Your hands are no longer beautiful?'

The fisher call, 'Bait, stack, store, repeat'
against the colour of the mackerel fleet.
She in shades, green, violet, blue,
wearing her colours lightly
to the steady breathing of the earth, the aphonic calm
with the mass of wild bees haloing the light
as you whacked me in the night.

I, the owner, had not found our lost dog,
found later dead, stuck in a bog.

At The Tableland

At the Tableland where it all began,
in god's muddy lanes and splashed thoughts,
his long road to introspection
and the creation of man,
went against his previous idea,
parked in a carport, of all things created
talking to one another, brother to brother.

Man held his talk quietly,
for the quiet calls the cool in the hot summer sun
when there was lots to ask in the summer green
of little Miss Goody Two Shoes, all homespun
with the herb sage in her hair
making pretty her countenance.

So when the opportunity came to suggest a sound
to the Swallow-tail butterfly, she could not understand,
nor I to reply. She flew her way and I went mine.

Probably, a bit early in the day for metaphysics
for the one that flew away
to the natural rhythms of wet and dry
and to god's unravelling polemics.

Salisbury Plain

In my land,
no one to work the land no more,
no one to cut the hedge after the thaw.
Although I'd been to this rodeo once before,
it was in a flop-house after dark
when a still started to fall from the Ark
and broncos ran mobs of camels in red dirt.
The Oz rainforest was cut to a desert.
O_2 dropped a diameter away, a disconcert
across a circle closed in a far way
Waun Mawn, in the Preseli Hills
where Merlin with his mob moved the stones to make the henge
on Salisbury Plain, to avenge
the red blood of the kill left to freeze in the chill.

In your land,
the wind went through the mixed blue grass
like a buffalo run, the Plains Apache's
ear against the ground feeling the violent sound
against his heart for what was to be the last time.
Last orders were called and the bell was rung in the bar,
'Time, gentlemen, please,' was the last he heard of sound.

Here, the stones were laid late that year,
following the absence, the drought of thought
and this and that. Pre-history delivers tat.
Who knows if we had a Maserati or two,
painted Apache red?

The Gauchos

In the summertime when the barley is high
and the night colours catch hues, slow scents,
a heron's feather trails from its fur
and mews a cry.

Transcendence goes beyond the element of chance
summer into an autumn trance.
I did not, at first, see something feral in you.
I saw the wonky knees, the smile
when open and large, the image
through my rose-coloured glasses.

On my bedside table in the Suriname hotel
a notice, 'No prostitutes allowed.'
Tell that to the gauchos in town for R+R,
then hit the bar, select a hostess for Sunday bliss.
Nice to be made at home.

I thought you were an animal kept in a cell.
An experiment, like a virus
but I did not realise you would mutate so fast
and that I would not last
to the autumn colours changing so fast.

There are songs which we sing that last,
and there are songs which we sing that do not last,
the truest friend does give nothing but hope,
otherwise god could come to a bad end.
Confess now, my old friend, it is winter's end.

I Have Been To A Place

I have been to a place where a magician lives
who no one has ever seen,
but he is known to change the shape of things,
of space, of time, of mass, the sung Latin Mass.

When I went to seek, along the long channel
flushed winter snow, with outflows
where spring primroses now grow, it seemed
everything comes here, the night owl early,
your lips to mine. Lilacs lost in cold change.

At first, I thought him a Green Man,
with primroses under his potter clay feet,
who would fill a pond with dew from a wind-blown cloud.
Or a Green Woman stained by a yew who burnt old wood
made of Dalradian schist,
settled well from stands, our hands touching
against the laurel standing like Rodin in mist.
Immovable like a great set Latin text
one is taught to recite to a magician,
who no one has ever seen.

San Francisco

In the St. Petersburg coffee houses
the intelligentsia were reading the Sunday newspapers
over croissants and cups of tea;
coffee considered too bourgeois in pre-revolutionary times.
In those days one read smoking a Havana cigar,
with white roses in a fresh white jar
and listened to a Catalan tune played on a Spanish guitar.

The Times carried an *esquisse*
by Karl Marx and Friedrich Engels,
written when there was an intelligentsia,
who would listen to Bach played on a clavier,
in the days before Thatcher and Trump.
The sketch proclaimed, 'The State is not "abolished",
it withers away.'
Might happen here some day, but not today.

In a San Francisco daydream
the redwoods gave out no sound, were still.
The shanty town with no style tried so hard
to be soft with feeling, like Perth W.A.
it had an orchestra and a mighty shrill.
It had massage parlours
to act as an antimacassar during happy hours.

It had hobos pushing supermarket carts
containing their life's work on a canvas of fine art.
Cassius Clay hitting with a potter's throw
marking the canvas of political thought
in a Turner water-colour, the hammer and sickle.

The first line of a sixties song went:

If you're going to San Francisco
be sure to wear some flowers in your hair.

Since medieval times there have been flowers
on the altar during Lent.
Before medieval times the redwoods flowered
in glorious splendour, no smog in the air.

The Bay is now written backwards
and inverted in a black ink script,
kept sealed in a gothic crypt.
No light in the San Francisco squalor,
for the hobos there is no mighty dollar.

If you're going to San Francisco,
be sure to time your visit in May
and take a dip in the polluted Bay.

It Is Mid March

It is mid March and the light is turning.
I always thought you looked more heathland,
heather in bloom, when the reed cutters came in
from a day's field work, the last straw still burning.

Your face to the west, on the turn,
your hands not the same,
as the church bell sounded through the leaves
on the breeze of late windburn.

A year of this pandemic.
The church hall has been dark for a year,
cold as a March hare, alone
in the remnants of Noah's flood.
This is not the way to rival Claude
or dismiss Weber's Protestant ethic,
thrown in a skip, to be placed in the cold earth,
when the purple heather popped.

Your face looked tense,
the red canary shouting loud
between a small condensed tone
and the solidity of the immense.

The flowers had different notes,
written in a different hand.

Wormwood

I always thought of you as from the Russian steppes,
a well-known bitter herb in Bible times
but you more cultivated in milder climes,
Artemisia absinthium or wormwood to me,
to be housed with the honey-bee in my skep.

In the book of Revelation
you were the name of a star
falling to earth from afar
to bitter the waters and cause desolation,
Chernobyl, Hiroshima, Nagasaki, Auschwitz.

As my father said 'Everyone needs a gimmick,'
but does it need to be so comic
to use the little phrase 'The final nail in the coffin'
dressed like a pixie in a fake bow tie
and walking with a stick like Charlie Chaplin.

It seems to be part of your psychology
to make a space after filling a space,
as a Proust line in French might say
hefted on the land to gain a sense of belonging.
Walking across the ice-cap,
with the melt snow behind a falling star.
Your music is old-fashioned,
as the pure angst of the last fandango showed,
a bitter-sweet taste the melt snow left behind.

Fingerpost Sign

I was wearing a pirate's ring
on the fingerpost lane in early spring,
when I saw a girl run down the hill
to the forest school, to the junction with no sign.

Hormones,
black hair and pink blush, the girl was in a rush,
with the design of passion in flowers, in the midday sun.
She ran the hill every step of the way.

The first aconites and snowdrops appeared
and the blackthorn swam in the Easter snow.
She was framed by a red bole
which gave the gold leaf a rich glow,
and she saw the whooper swan fly over
the fingerpost sign, but not the van.

And I thought of Judge Jeffreys out to dine
at *The Mayflower,* on the Thames, drinking his wine,
watching the pirates he had sentenced drown
on a rising spring tide at sundown.

III

They Waved White Handkerchiefs

The waved white handkerchiefs on the Berlin wall,
like the orang-utan with pressed hands on the JCB
to stop it uproot his tree
both buttressed by so much sophistry in a thrown snowball.

The frogspawn was contaminated that year:
tailless black dots on a music score,
arranged by Scriabin
who knew as much about orchestration
as a pig about oranges, as Shostakovich made clear.
Can you catch a scattered mind, my dear?

The frogspawn had dried. The orang-utan had died.
The snowballs were rolling along curved space,
against a grey tundra sky and you wheyface,
in a kimono the colour of peat,
gave me a woman's kiss on a woman.
The worst sense is of a solitary spring
in a painting by Vermeer
when the north-easterlies rush a clear cold
through the lines of limes
and white handkerchiefs are waved in fear.

The Great US of A

Visited once, there was not much to say
about the place where they corral the call girls
in a wagon wheel, black girls with a rope
lassoed around white pricks.
It seemed like a movie made in Tangiers,
or Casablanca with Bogart and Co
all having one too many beers,
when life draws away and China comes out to play.

America what is your womb
but a big bomb and a massive balloon?
Yep, you boys do bullshit strong,
I know it sucks when you size it down South
to the Mississippi dirt poor black girls
caught in the headlight of a President
who gropes girls' parts, mirrored in the headlight
as he departs after one term.

It was not known after Lincoln died
what was to come, but one came to trump them all
and fail at the time of the roll-call.

Visited once, never again
to see the Mississippi poor and so many more.
But rich white kids don't give a fig
as long as they can make the almighty dollar big.

I Was Once Asked

I was once asked if all women were prostitutes
connected as they are to Eve, made to conceive
for little else, to provide a small piece.
Shostakovich's female denouncing the State on the piano stage;
a Russian girl licking the wallpaper paste
as the Nazis tried to enter the gate in Leningrad.
A Russian girl with nothing in the grate, just a dead rat
and a piece of slate, chalk and mis-talk,
her piano smashed for firewood beside the grate.

You were always that little girl, back not straight
leaning over the piano keys, fingering articulated
around the clock, ticking at eight o'clock.
Did you finger the keys to marry right,
to money and power, love on one side?
For a man, love is a different thing,
hence the ring given in Leningrad
by the view of an open sea, for you and me,
in that brief moment of false delight.

Sorry, not true, not all women are so polite
as to offer a finger and behave in this way.
But, ultimately, some do.
When the juice is back from the press,
and memory is filtered, you had no care from where.
You, who went to the Leningrad green sea
to use the two hundred year old cider press,
to press you to me and confess the sour apple juice
left no distance against a fallacy on your breath.

Prostitutes do not grow on trees,
or come in one, two or threes
in the Willow Tea Rooms, segregated.
The working class to the bottom floor, unkempt.
You exempt, no prostitute in that Leningrad fog
watching a slip of breeze score a winter
ripple to move in a certain way,
the spoken word in freeze, all destitute.

On The Eve Of A December Divorce

At the beginning, a marriage offers hope
listening to Tallis
offering no fallacy, no false promises
said when the flowers were bursting
vitality in full bloom and opened trails,
thoughts and feelings during
a long marriage to the end.

December, so short on time,
lengthens the day.
It's not nice to spend a day with a cat on the kill,
to feel her shake at the back of the neck
and reflect why Beethoven liked the C minor key
when he was young, with titanium white
and his gun against the door
to prevent the end; his brevity in yellow ochres
lightening the mood,
like mixing nuclear plutonium, white powder
in talk about being free.

Zola played the same game,
a zero-sum game, to close the door
and keep me shut away.
A bad dream, I as a schmuck performed.
She preferred the Italianate Baroque
with Milstein playing Bach against the clock,
with swirls against her skirts, up and down
as in a bad dream of what was to become;
the cracks in the masonry.

The weight of the church when I said, 'I do'
and then the whack of the birch
to hope and an open view. Closure.
The end, when you said, 'I don't.'

In The Leningrad Ice

In the Leningrad ice comrades would strip the wallpaper,
the dried glue licked by thin red lips. Lunch.
Recycling their waste during the siege
by dead bodies iced over during the freeze.

At that time, Eton schoolboys would dress
as Red Indians at play for their annual ball
in costumes designed to conceal a fat paunch,
rich and overfed as Leningrad bled.

A mixed up bundle of string unravelled
by a black rat sniffing a dead body.
Capitalism may not be the thing
but what have we got left in an empty tin?

The wallpaper looked so grand to the petit bourgeoisie
in rich damask red woven into tiny threads.
The Eton boys still at play in their glee
after a full tea, the servants dismissed
to iced attic rooms to stare at bare walls
and think of the Leningrad dead.

After all, Eton boys were simply being trained
to express Capitalism's white lies.
In Leningrad they only had red lies for bread.
Fate decides who lives and who dies
but I'd never met an alchemist before
who could change Leningrad into St. Petersburg.
Communism into Capitalism, both buried in concrete
around Chernobyl. We've got to move on,
maybe to the Tiber and have jam for tea.

In Vogue

As the pendulum swings recording the passage of time
and the changes in design,
everything comes back into fashion.
Fascists. *Vogue.*
I must look at the latest front cover,
under the toilet seat and in the bowl,
when I get off the lav to have a fag
and sit down again to look at the cover.
My dad used to take the *Daily Express,*
now I take *Vogue* to regress
and to reflect on the disparity between you and me.

On the front cover a possible spelling mistake,
a gene gone wrong?
An anorexic girl in a long slit skirt
pouts at me. One the back cover
an ad. for a Paris perfume,
as I get off the seat and flush the bowl clean
and leave the room in gloom,
to switch on the circuit breaker.

All Lives Matter In A Fancy Dress

End Black Lives Matter with words that matter
in gothic thoughts held up by a scaffold,
a meaningless jingle raddled.
With freckled thinking I thought we are what we are
in the spring time,
in the summer time,
in the autumn time,
in the black winter time.
We are what we are any time.

Squinted slogans like scrambled chatter
imprint words which serve only to batter,
in stone for when you return home
to drop the baby in the sea,
my mother and me learning to straighten
the algorithm, whilst listening to Prokofiev's sarcasm.

What are those notes falling on the crest?
Waves of thoughts come home to nest,
the rainbow arc, black against a mummering.

All lives matter in a fancy dress.

From The Muddy Pond

From the muddy pond of ideas,
splashed across the face and cheek
turned away, what can I say?
You were wrong to speak, protected from original sin,
carried out in the dustman's bin.
You did say to me in Peckham that day
you did not wish to stray,
from Goya's prints fat and rich
slimmed down by the dog and bitch.

Let's forget the *mañana* option
from the woman in a half-fitted wig,
with her half-fitted idea to cause disruption
killing T-cells, tweaked to kick you out.
Not giving a fig about cancel culture,
anchored in myth and mankind,
Chopin mazurkas written to be unkind
in a nostalgia of finding hidden flowers,
or koalas in the bushfires.

With the bleakness of the Gulag still lingering,
writers, authors, lawyers, white
enemies of the State, none were black,
but felt hate as slaves in the mines.
Overworked, beaten and starving they were white.

That day you made a big splash in the muddy pond
and the tide was ebbing on slack water,
I pulled a trick with the dolly bird;
you thought I was absurd to face the rock
and match the colour on the cliff.
'Beware of rockfalls,' you said, with a musical hum.

From Leicester To Aberdeen

From Leicester to Aberdeen a twelve hour trip
but onward I was always taken to Peterhead
to see the scratched names of the dead
surrounded by the shanty sound flax flat
in the trodden straw ground.
The graves for the lowest rank decreed
by the bottom feeders of a society born
of a storm, as I saw on the scratch given to the poor.

At first I was five, then seven, then ten
taken again and again to Peterhead
and I learnt it was Peterheed.

It was in a deep lake I lost the ring
for evermore, a lost magic wand
when I caught my dish.
I picked out the flax in her Saxon hair
with the fleas and over the years, long years
of the sickle and red cross and CND
what mattered most her or me?
But it was not to be.

Robben Island, South Africa

In the spring, that stretching space of time,
the bamboo was bundled into sticks, ready
for the Autumn time, when mother could clothe
herself in her piece of paradise,
in finely knit sewed stitch, which she together
loosely missed the lost stitch.

She picked the piece, lost, and lost
left alone she and me together, talked of sin
of a mistaken bloom as she unstitched the bundle
on the stone floor and chose the bamboo stick.

I watched the mummy ape hit the stick
against the mulberry tree and then test me.
Bitterness is indeed a turn of kind in one's own mind
for want of a thing far, far better.
Maybe a mandala circle,
a strive for the Jungian unity: the self complete.

For Mandela, the jailor's stick beat the drum,
as on Mandela's long walk he sought his universe
and asked the Buddhist nun for his nirvana day.

The litany of terror to be put in reverse.
Sharpeville, 1960. The Pass Laws.
The hunger strikes. The tortured to death.
Hard labour in the lime quarry, no shoes allowed.
The ear of corn, stream in flood; the shibboleth.
The treatment of man on man.
Four visits a year, thirty minutes long.
Four censored letters a year.

Fretful sleep on a concrete floor,
listening to the winter winds, for eighteen years.

Mother, you can bundle back your bamboo sticks.
I still think of Mandela and of his jailor's kicks.

Fit For Whistler's Brush

Fit for Whistler's brush: low sun over the marsh,
kind light freezing harsh
to blitz the hard blow when the dark clouds come
in a smell of turpentine in a sufi swirling trance.

The sacred geometry in the power of script:
the call to prayer,
in a Latinized text to reinforce ideology
of a male folly to write words in water.

Cursive in your thoughts, your curves were not
long ignored, in particular your wonky knees,
and your dialect, like a water splash
on a stone wall.

Becoming my muse turned out to be bad news.
In the Beethoven Cello sonata
you were always faithful to the text,
a mixed Jew playing the chords pro rata.

We have three spires at Lichfield, that is true
but we are a nation gone askew.
Ethical consumerism to a global brand
forced by the EU to shape our hand.

A brown salt glaze dipped in a de-couple,
you were a pantomime dame we could boo.
Go fuck you, EU
to me you were always untrue.

The Poor Little Things

The poor little things didnae ken
growing up in Peckham about seeds lost
hundreds of years ago,
disturbed to grow anew in a bubble all sken.

Dark and dank when that little seed sank,
the poor little things didnae ken
how to grow their religion open.
How could they know slitting throats was wrong?
Or pulling a thong to one side
for the hymen to be caught on the school gate,
distracted by such a silly idea
of being a virgin bride to a desert catch
and become the wonder of femininity,
the way shadows lose their colour and virginity
according to the light
and her dark grey metamorphic rock of hate.

Just pull your thong to one side
for the hymen hurt will be less
than piercing an eye for a virgin bride.
After all, beliefs recede according to the level of stress.

In Crieff they made the green leaf into black tea
when little babies thin at all their joints
were fattened up in light and shade
and pricked with sharp leaves, green in desert sands
at Rogation time. What do you want,
a divine chorus as you put on your schoolgirl skirt
to forget your hurt?

Listen to the ice waters of St. Petersburg
and not the howl of the desert sands sound.
Taste the black tea with me. I may not be bright
but do not wash my religion in bright sunlight
or know of my absolute right.

I can do perspective too, look at Leonardo
before you pierce an eye or two.
Stretch your hymen in a different way
not on such a silly idea
to be a schoolgirl virgin bride.

Before drinking the black tea, infused
with ideas of making Christians dead,
perhaps you should have thought of that desert sand
under the horses with trumpeters on top
of an adoration of the magi.
Before drinking the black tea, confused in a fog
adoring a dark fake, seeking a schoolgirl rape
under the varnish of the green desert tree.

The poor little things didnae ken
why so many religions were born in deserts.
Deserts of ideas and humanity,
worn behind the black veil of vanity.
Her dialectic confused me,
three kids after the hymen split
wanting back to the land of the infidel Brit.
Why be a cry-baby now? With blended learning
find your place in Shoreditch,
where they used to throw dead dogs in the ditch.
Why not stay with your desert clan
and posture through your lawyer your vile élan?
When thundersnow hit Crieff and exposed
your false grief as you sipped black tea.

You poor little thing,
read the tealeaves in a different way.
Principles need to be translated into rules
and on the basis of your own rules
you need to burn.

Some Time Ago

Some time ago I went to Morocco
and tasted the last olive before the sand,
travelled the highest pass in the Atlas Mountains,
ate meat and potatoes in a beaten dough
in search of a promised land.

It was strange, like my first fervour unmasked
by another name in the dyeing vats.
The women hanging cloth on lines unasked,
the dye dripping fat onto the garden wall
made from BP cans to enclose paradise,
safe from the sands.

When in the sand to find self-sacrifice,
the pauses became longer and more intense
between each breath, more dense, more nomadic,
the sound of the sand more melodic.
As we are cemented in property and the rest.

No promised land but a single olive tree
and a strange feeling on the back of my neck
as your teeth made their bite, cat-like.
It felt like a panther girl in December snow
with lots of memories and now no glow.

The Travelling Van

The travelling van was timed the German way,
precisely.
Five minutes forty seconds to send them on their way.
Unfortunately for the guards in the last minute
or two the inmates dropped their discharge on the floor
to create work for more, clearing the shit.
But what do you expect from Jews to affect a shift?

She had no moisturising cream to use on her hands
to soften the sounds before entering the chamber.
Her hands undone, cold cream would have done,
thicker to soften the sounds.

But her arm was torn by the guard-room door
a Shepherd dog, tore and tore, to wrench her entrance
to the chamber room where she with another
went into an embrace,
so strong that in that universe black hole
where I had belonged she went into another song
when they applied the vanishing cream
to kill her life's dream.

Swampy

I have missed you.
I tried to eat a vole tunnelling underground
like a mole; I'm not a veggie man.
More, I thought, an also-ran.
I could not swing through the trees
as an orang-utan,
or fight the swelkie and wax the moon
as a partisan, to cover and protect.

When in Orkney, underground,
I missed you this evening of my great delight.
I missed you, my miss of the night.
I missed you, my virgin of the night,
from the men who drew the sense of war,
who tried to wash away your sense of awe.
Our ancient woodlands to be cut through
with a *Stihl* chainsaw.

Five thousand years of mistakes;
the wasted, spent years.
I thought of the gunnera planted so carefully
by the sea, as the great freeze whitewashed
the Cold War greyness.
The nuclear submarine leaving its chamber tomb,
under a snow moon; a chimera poxed with gonorrhoea.

I see you now in a carnival mirror reflection,
emerge after a thirty day tunnel
under Euston Square to stop HS2.
With unbranded eloquence, you can only try
to see the light and find what is true.

Last Minute Kabuki

Last minute Kabuki for the bothy boys
wallowing in a sea loch lined with oysters,
the texture tacit, milky totemic
for bothy boys catching Loch Fyne salmon,
in a matter of tribe called a clan, he the he-man
talking fake news for the bothy boys.

A Scottish sea loch is a dangerous place
for Jocks who have lost their sense of place.
A German philosopher once said
that the road to totalitarianism
is paved between the cracks of saying
what is true to be untrue.
The SNP, all blue and white, pulled off a coup
grabbing votes by a Bannockburn moat
and a sea long for the bothy boys
to watch Kabuki for a minute or two
but fishing for red herring had them caught in a trap,
more real is to hate.
Hate the English to a podium clap, clap, clap.
Half Scottish, half English I tried to tell
what the bothy boys didnae ken.

Her Chemistry

Her chemistry was best when she pulled
the magic pin from the grenade,
as the red squirrel, so scarce to see these days
ran along the colonnade
and climbed up the apple blossom tree
to register at Scot Blood.
Bannockburn in Black Death times.

As Kierkegaard said, 'One becomes the thing,'
and the red squirrel stored her limes
and ate her ferns.
You became the thing: the smell of the marrow
lingering on the morrow, with that narrow
jackass of an idea
as a matinée idol stores a dream,
smoke screened in a church at night, by moonlight.

We reach each other through touch
when speech ends, or begins.
We touched the stored dream
as we watched the red squirrel by moonbeam.

Be still my heart, the fruit will come
in its own season and carry its zeitgeist spirit
to form a thought and feel.

Masai

The Masai danced with the elephant in the room
to a crazy tune, when I did not see
too far down the road to decolonize
and modernize the colours of Africa,
and show the open.

Instead, they swarmed like screaming pihas
against the door,
to a walking base with a Baroque trope,
the rolling C-base within a little coda,
leaving little hope
for the elephant in the room
plodding around the African plain.

Let's speak of the matter of the day,
on those broad bands across the plain.
The flint church stitched by a day witch
into the colours of Africa, with a quick switch
of a bible for social exchange theory,
a new trafficker; the elephant in the room.

The Masai make a good fire, you can hear the wood tick.
We make a bad fire, you can hear the wood spitz.

She Took A Mazy Run

She took a mazy run like a redneck unspun,
onto something other than the banal,
where there is no sun.
With hanging breasts and a pot belly
and a voice, ethereal she sung.
But what songs she sang.

Popeye exchanged his pork-pie hat
for Popeye the sailor man, his French connection
flattened out his vowels,
he spent hours and hours on pronunciation.
Until, 'Hey luv, put on a brew,'
became, 'My darling, shall we take tea?'
in a new teflon song in mint tea; a new evaluation.

She used to pick cotton in the US South,
until Trump washed out her mouth
and her song went on a mazy run,
in the deep Southern sun.

Grenfell Tower

I had lived in a tower block
twenty storeys high
and in a power cut had watched the candle die.
So now, watching on early morning TV
the people who came here to escape
a place in the sun,
from the backwaters of Bangkok
or from the heat of Bangladesh,
huddled together behind a door locked
because the advice was to remain still.
The smell of burnt flesh confined
in a flat clad in fear,
as a lone woman walks at night
toward an orange glow,
and thinks an unthinkable thought
clad in a candle light,
that spring cannot now be denied,
as a moth is drawn to a candle flame.
The endgame.

IV

Good Friday

The four rivers of life come alive
with the spring sunshine and a surprise,
the plod use a baton to baton the head
and have a neo-Nazi in their ranks,
aren't they all?

The Easter sunshine shone the stained glass
depicting the baton used to get ahead.
The plod came from a pod of an indifferent idea
that Jesus carried with him to the cross.
Thorns around his head, the baton laid to dead,
wrapped in a golden fleece.

When a neo-Nazi nailed his baton
to the monastery door and ripped down all
in the physic garden before the fall.
When they took the monastery down
there was no symmetry between the flowers
either side of the cross; two cold sides
cleaned with sea salt and lemon
and one neo-Nazi in their ranks
drove the nails into the hands.

Anton Webern

A mummy's boy, Schumann caught in a frock of distress,
Webern in mummy's dress.
The umbilical cord not quite cut right by an imbecile
to an atonal feel.
The wind going through the trees in high tones;
the note-row stunted, fly-blown
part-notes, part sounds serially unlinked,
out of sync, as in the open concentration camps.
The inmates clinging to an iceberg
to form a palindrome rehearsed at Nuremberg,
where not in casual style,
the notes wrote only once.

Returning To Leicester

The pews had been sawed in half to fit the bar.
Still and numbered still, allotted
for the imbibers in for a quick jar.
Placed lounge lizard style, red cushions on top
as neat as a cardinal's red hat, calotted.

Who sawed in half our once true faith,
whored, tore out the silent stillness
paradise can provide in belief?
A god enshrined in an architectural style,
a gothic god decorated in a pigsty.

Henry VIII and Cardinal Wolsey
ate their croissants and drank their ale
and marked their pew with a single cross,
indifferent to their infidelity,
of the decaying world of the red rot,
the rotting heartwood, of god's dropped anchor.
For their idea was a sure thing, a real banker.
To break with Rome and go it alone
and fatten the pig.

Silks From The Fallen Ship

Silks from the fallen ship
having caught a wave from an angel's breath
did rip the Van Dyck brown sail to cause her death
and spread her memory in the water meadows of cowslip.

You can always trust a household name
although it is never played each time the same
as when I heard Ravel's *Sonatine*, the *animé*
sound like Durkheim's anomie.
The malady of an infinite suicide spilled as roadkill
now at the tipping point still.

Van Dyck brown holds a lot of paint in the brush
as applied to the salt glaze
when the fallen ship in outrush
lost in a maze of anomie and increasingly remote time.

Francis Bacon

From the lost world of the Anglo-Irish Ascendancy
he never claimed he would save souls,
or make almost men vainglorious,
seeing his work show a certain tendency
to question the usual terms and conditions,
stuck with ticket-tout software for the curious.

I always believed his stand was on the question of morality
and with a ferocious otherness
to reveal the bit of feral in our supposed liberality.
We are all animals dressed up in a different fashion
pretending to bathe in Christ's compassion.

Several years ago we were a virus too
and he, the hunter, to trap the virus in transience.
When we became animal and a liar,
he became an *animalier,* to speak true;
to catch with bared teeth, tear apart
and think on you.

So She Went To Her Cave

So she went to her cave where the music scores stayed
she, umbilically attached, cello to babe.
Jacqueline du Pré.
The day before she died I prayed
to a god whose previous joke played
like a Schubert song.

I picture him as an East End geezer,
a right bloke, who goes for broke,
no time for the A-major cello sonata Beethoven wrote.

Played incidentally by Barenboim and du Pré.
But, I forgot you made Beethoven hum in deaf,
another of your little jokes.

Perhaps, you are constantly as high as a kite on coke,
while between your fingers you spin the world.
Jokes are good to hear, until they misfire.

We Live On A Land Between The Seas

We live on a land between the seas;
a fair isle conceived by a god
running on the spot when Europe got too hot.
Jews burnt nicely that cold night,
god running on the spot, crunching bones
in his hands to make a heap of ash alight.

It was the time the atheist had truly come.
Was god just turning ash into cash,
whilst listening to Liszt out on the piss,
to a tune that could be hummed?
One more cremated Jewess increases income, after all.

The ash trees have die-back now,
their slender, cleanly curving limbs
sprout silvery shoots that drop now
and curl up like branches of a chandelier,
to cross the t's and dot the i's
of your legacy coated in a lustrous sheen,
of running on the spot in an ash veneer,
as diverse as red and black,
until now, largely unseen, will be on your plaque.

The louts and the bully boys shout a lot,
to make money they strip the bark.
After all, stripping Jews to watch them burn
is just a lark.

We live on a land between the seas,
where between the mountains and the lough
it is primaeval to forage, to fish the sea.

God, stop running on the spot
and place your head on the butcher's block,
as we watch the chop split the log.
The Jewess waited for the slow match strike,
god, who told you, you were such a catch?
But I'm with the feminists who thought you a perfect dyke,
running on the spot.

After Schubert

The beehive on top of the cathedral
held the bee with the bright blue light
bringing in new beginnings in musty
incense song mixed in smells of citral.

How TV music has touched our lives forever.
Roll over Schubert asleep in your bed. Forget Beethoven
with his long bars whiplashed in the tonic key,
played in a lounge in Samarkand
where you picked out a phrase in Latin verse
which remained an illusion. Notes written in water.

I saw this man in a penguin suit
nervously walk on to the stage
to play Schubert sonatas for what seemed like an age,
the music was strangely mute.

Let us fly with the notes this night.
I say I love you, you say you love me
and we wait for connectivity to be.
So why scold me once more for extinguishing
the bright blue light from your bee?

Open

To drown in Venice, as is found
to go the way of poetry not sound
amber with a gold colour around the end
with a Welsh preacher, an undertaker by profession,
pinned on a board like a butterfly or moth
to look for open skies
and chance on four or fives.

Come on man, you do him with a sledge
and bury him in a thick hedge
a lump of black fur on the stair
containing your preacher hiding in the black
behind the door religion. Closed in Venice,
and I wrote your name in green ink
to make the Catholic church think.

I Always Liked Georgian Architecture

I always liked Georgian architecture,
a funny mix between Gaelic psalm singing
and the stained-glass lancet window
dressed in the wet grey stone.

She played the black notes as a cat
out at night, looking for mischief
and the white notes quiet.
Schumann's *Phantasiestücke* with nuance
and grace, holding a white handkerchief
between the bars.

She looked like Mikhail Tal, the nose, the jaw,
the claws on the keys; the pecking jackdaw
worrying the golden mean, Mariam Batsashvili
the Georgian with air around the sound
of the allyship.
White Russians lost the war, after all
to create a society with a harelip.

Leicester

Why God did you give us Jesus,
malaria, SARS, mumps and the flu,
when you knew, after the daily grind
we would never know a glaucous with a waxy bloom?

I've heard the phrase big-headed bastard before,
but that was in Leicester where precision is lightly
engineered, an afterthought. Was he late thought?
God, I would have thought you had told your son
to vaccinate the vaccinators first
before he vaccinated us all with his thoughts.

In Leicester I knew a dancing queen,
a wannabe Trump lie, to my never-been.
Arms and needles and good behaviour
did not prevent a grubby city reject a saviour.
Big-headed bastards lined Leicester streets.
Tell Thatcher society does exist,
spray the flies and make them cry, pull their wings.
Why choose to divorce in December cold,
Jesus, why hit with such a hard fist?

With Tallis Counting His Latin Notes

With Tallis counting his Latin notes
in ones, twos and threes
and you all dressed up to recite,
with an open voice, all of one in semaphore.
It seems does become to fall the tone
as we extoll and enrol his majesty.

The three Marys to the west of Innisfree
did unsettle Schubert's smile and bring darkness,
deeply entangled in the resignation of late Brahms
to the tune of the honey-bee,
as I fell into your arms.
Schumann said, 'Let the *Well-Tempered Clavier*
be your daily bread.'

The three Marys to the west of Innisfree
declined in dark, dystopian times
but instead read Yeats's poetry
and gave one minute's thought
that words grew no flowers and left for the fallow time.

The soundscape still that is November
open for all to view. The rush of the sea
through the throwing leaves I still remember.
A soundscape in a landscape no longer green;
the three Marys' gifts were a penance,
my atonement for Schubert's lean song,
wrought by me all wrong.